Copyright 2020 Stephen Gamlin. All rights reserved. No part of this book may be reproduced or transmitted in any form or by any means, electronic or mechanical, including photocopying, recording, scanning or by an information storage and retrieval system – except by a reviewer who may quote brief passages in a review to a printed magazine, newspaper or on the Web – without permission in writing from the author.

For more information, please visit https://www.MotivationalFirewood.com or send an e-mail to Steve@SteveGamlin.com

The author, editor and publisher have made every attempt to secure the most accurate and correct information for quotations herein. Any inaccuracies or errors are unintentional. First printing 2009.

ATTENTION CORPORATIONS, UNIVERSITIES, COLLEGES AND PROFESSIONAL ORGANIZATIONS: Quantity discounts are available on bulk purchases of this book for education, gifts or as premiums for increasing magazine subscriptions or renewals. For more information, please contact Steve@SteveGamlin.com

ISBN: 978-0-9767993-3-7

Dedication

This book is dedicated to everyone in my life who has inspired a smile, a laugh and a great feeling in my heart.

Some are family. Some are close friends. Many were strangers.

Without all of you, I would not be me.

Thank you very much for encouraging me to create and enjoy this remarkable experience.

You have all made this world a better place.

An extra-special dedication goes to Tina, the love of my life, who has been the greatest gift of all.

I love you...very very.

Contents

1. It All Starts With Intention
2. The Most Important Meal of the Day
3. Reach Out and Re-Touch Someone
4. Hold That Door!
5. R-E-L-A-X
6. Remember Our Furry Friends
7. Tolls for Two
8. Make Yourself Rich
9. Good Cause, Great Rewards
10. Special Delivery
11. Words are Worth a Thousand Pictures
12. Enjoy Thanksgiving Every Day
13. Have a Laugh!
14. Get Back in the Game
15. Park It Right Here
16. Don't Keep the Change
17. Share Your Expertise
18. The Gift of Music
19. The Power of Praise
20. Capture the Moment, Make It Last Forever

Introduction

*The title of this book is "20 to Life".
Sounds like a prison sentence, doesn't it?
It very well may be one.
Yours!*

Can you name at least one person in your life you would describe as…hmm, how should I say it…*negative*?

You may already be serving a life sentence, frantically swimming against a tide of negative people who surround you: family, friends, co-workers, society. All it takes is a glance at the evening news or a quick skim through the first few headlines of an internet news site and there it is, just waiting to flush your good mood down the toilet…if you let it.

Want to plan your escape?

No matter where you are in the world or in your own heart, the simple fact that you have opened this book tells me there is something wonderful about you. At this moment, you are investing in yourself, which is the best investment you will ever make.

I like you already.

Your life may already be spectacular. If it is, congratulations! This is the perfect reminder of your opportunity to share that light with others. Or you may feel stuck in a rut the size of the Grand Canyon, surrounded by sheer cliffs of negativity.

Anyone can have a bad day, be jostled by a dip in the road, or feel stuck.

The world is not a perfect place. We are not always smiling. It is what you *choose* to do at these times that can make all the difference in the world for yourself and those around you: family, friends, co-workers, even complete strangers. Who knows? Your smile and simple action may just inspire others who really need a boost in their day, week, month or life. You could be a hero to *that* person, who may then take action of his/her own to inspire yet another.

See how this can work?

This book describes twenty simple actions you can take to make the world a better place for yourself and maybe even for someone else. Some require only a moment of your time, some take a bit longer. Read through them. Find the ones that resonate with your personal style. Commit them in any order you like.

Every page of the book carries the opportunity to create a smile and a refreshing, positive boost in your mood and attitude. You may wish to jot your results on the Success Pages, which can re-trigger that same smile and good feeling down the road.

When you are done with the book, you may wish to start over again and involve even more people. Share it with your family. Share it with a friend. Share it with the world.

I want to sincerely thank you, from the bottom of my heart, for selecting this little book as part of your personal development library.

Best wishes to you as you take a new step, every day, in your life's journey.

Sincerely,

1

It All Starts With Intention

"A person's true wealth is the good he does in this world."
- Mohammed

Whenever your day begins, this step can get you up on the right side of the bed.

As soon as your eyes are able to focus, look in the mirror.

Point at your reflection, tap your heart, look yourself in the eye and say with conviction:

"You, my friend, are going to make something very positive happen today… for yourself, and for at least one other person."

Genuinely anticipate and feel the emotions that will come from accomplishing this simple goal.

Begin thinking of something you can do, even the smallest gesture, to bring this statement to fruition.

Take this first step today, and every day!

Actions and Results (The Success Stories)

Date: _____ Action: _____
Result: _____
_____
_____

Date: _____ Action: _____
Result: _____
_____
_____

Date: _____ Action: _____
Result: _____
_____
_____

Date: _____ Action: _____
Result: _____
_____
_____

Date: _____ Action: _____
Result: _____
_____

2

The Most Important Meal of the Day

"A learned man has always wealth in himself."
- Latin Proverb

This phrase is often used to describe breakfast which, depending upon your tastes, can range from healthy yogurt and fruit to a heart-challenging stack of syrup-drizzled pancakes flanked by a plate of bacon, sausage, eggs and hash browns.

I have enjoyed both.

I believe the most important meal of the day is the one that jump-starts your mind and heart. All too often, we wake in the morning and immediately seek the TV news or social media.

What is there for us? Violence, tragedy, negativity, doom and gloom. Is it important to be informed? Yes. Do we need to bathe in so much negativity? In my opinion: no!

If you can, set your alarm clock fifteen minutes earlier than usual, and spend that time reading something that will add value to your life.

Learn something new about your career field. Read about the wonderful things people are doing in the world to help others.

Feed positive messages to your mind and heart!

Actions and Results (The Success Stories)

Date: _____ Action: _____
Result: _____
_____
_____

Date: _____ Action: _____
Result: _____
_____
_____

Date: _____ Action: _____
Result: _____
_____
_____

Date: _____ Action: _____
Result: _____
_____
_____

Date: _____ Action: _____
Result: _____
_____

3

Reach Out and Re-Touch Someone

"What is a friend? A single soul dwelling in two bodies."
- Aristotle

For most of us, the world is a very busy place. Work, home, family, bills, activities…the calendar is full.

After a while it can become a blur. Old friends often fall by the wayside, replaced by the nameless, faceless hum of daily life.

But all is not lost. You've still got the great memories and stories, so why not take five minutes to check in with someone and re-live one of them?

Break out your old address book and make a list of the people you miss. Try a web search if you need to find them. Jot a little note next to each name.

That way, if you go to voicemail, you can quickly leave a few words about a great memory you shared with that person.

It might take a minute, but it could improve your whole day.

It can have the same impact for the person you are calling too!

Reconnect with someone special today.

Actions and Results (The Success Stories)

Date: _____ Action: _____
Result: _____
_____
_____

Date: _____ Action: _____
Result: _____
_____
_____

Date: _____ Action: _____
Result: _____
_____
_____

Date: _____ Action: _____
Result: _____
_____
_____

Date: _____ Action: _____
Result: _____
_____

4

Hold That Door!

"Wherever there is a human being, there is an opportunity for a kindness."
- Seneca

For anyone who has ever been on the receiving end of a closed door you *thought* was going to be held open (as you struggled with an armful of boxes), you know what I mean.

Want to make someone's life a little easier? Hold a door open.
My town's post office and bank share a building, and it is not uncommon for someone to hold a door for five or six people.

I watch daily as smiles and laughter mix with genuine appreciation for the person who has taken the time to execute this simple gesture of kindness.

For children, it sets a very good example. For adults, it conveys an important reminder: We are *never* too busy to have good manners and help our fellow citizens.

What doors could you hold open today?

Actions and Results (The Success Stories)

Date: _____ Action: _____
Result: _____
_____
_____

Date: _____ Action: _____
Result: _____
_____
_____

Date: _____ Action: _____
Result: _____
_____
_____

Date: _____ Action: _____
Result: _____
_____
_____

Date: _____ Action: _____
Result: _____
_____

5

R-E-L-A-X

"Health is the soul that animates all the enjoyments of life, which fade and are tasteless without it."
- William Temple

When was the last time you treated yourself to a massage? The therapeutic effects (physical, mental, and emotional) of such attention on your neck, shoulders, back, and feet can be amazing.

If you are in a relationship, perhaps you can arrange a trade of massage time with your partner.

Power down your phone, turn off the television, light a candle, select your favorite soothing music, tune out the rest of the world, and enjoy.

Or, if your budget allows, schedule time with a professional massage therapist. Even a fifteen-minute chair massage (perfect for those who are a bit on the shy side) can work wonders.

Enjoy a taste of relaxation today!

Actions and Results (The Success Stories)

Date: _____ Action: _____
Result: _____
_____
_____

Date: _____ Action: _____
Result: _____
_____
_____

Date: _____ Action: _____
Result: _____
_____
_____

Date: _____ Action: _____
Result: _____
_____
_____

Date: _____ Action: _____
Result: _____
_____

6

Remember Our Furry Friends

"Any glimpse into the life of an animal quickens our own and makes it so much the larger and better in every way."
- John Muir

In almost every community, there are organizations dedicated to caring for a wide variety of animals.

In veterinary offices, animal shelters and rescue leagues, dedicated professionals (typically accompanied by numerous volunteers) often provide twenty-four-hour care for our friends of the animal world.

Want to feel great?

Find one in your area today and ask how you can help. Perhaps they could benefit from some clean blankets, a bag of dog food, newspapers or a few containers of cat litter.

Who knows?

You may even get to pet a goat, help brush a horse or be the *very* special person who gently places a new 'best friend' in the waiting hands of a child.

Actions and Results (The Success Stories)

Date: _____ Action: _____
Result: _____
_____
_____

Date: _____ Action: _____
Result: _____
_____
_____

Date: _____ Action: _____
Result: _____
_____
_____

Date: _____ Action: _____
Result: _____
_____
_____

Date: _____ Action: _____
Result: _____
_____

7

Tolls for Two

"You have not lived until you have done something for someone who can never repay you."
- Anonymous

Over the last few years, I have noticed that most highway tollbooths now use an electronic gadget to save time and keep traffic flowing more effectively.

Being a procrastinator, I am still using the one remaining lane that contains a human being, which allows me to regularly commit the following act.

Several times a month, as I pull up, I hold out an extra dollar and inform the attendant: "Hi, I'm also paying for my friend behind me!"

As I pull forward slowly, I often glance in the mirror to see the confused look on that driver's face, which quickly changes to a smile and a shared laugh with the attendant.

For a dollar, I have just made three people smile.

Looking for a safe investment in *any* market?

This is a sure winner!

Actions and Results (The Success Stories)

Date: _____ Action: _____
Result: _____
_____
_____

Date: _____ Action: _____
Result: _____
_____
_____

Date: _____ Action: _____
Result: _____
_____
_____

Date: _____ Action: _____
Result: _____
_____
_____

Date: _____ Action: _____
Result: _____
_____

8

Make Yourself Rich

"The Possible's slow fuse is lit by the imagination."
- Emily Dickinson

This action originally started with an accidental double-tap at an ATM machine. As I was rushing to make a deposit, I intended to enter $100 but apparently hit the zero button a couple extra times.

When I looked down, I suddenly realized I was about to make a deposit of $10,000. Wow!

I am willing to bet that the hidden camera caught the biggest smile it had seen all day. As there was nobody waiting behind me, I took an extra moment to envision the day when I actually will be making deposits like this on a regular basis.

Still smiling, I *felt* the feelings that I will have when that day comes. It actually triggered ideas of how I can make this future possible.

Try this enriching action today for yourself.

REMINDER: Be sure to cancel the process so that you can re-enter your deposit with the *correct* amount!

Actions and Results (The Success Stories)

Date: _____ Action: _____
Result: _____
_____
_____

Date: _____ Action: _____
Result: _____
_____
_____

Date: _____ Action: _____
Result: _____
_____
_____

Date: _____ Action: _____
Result: _____
_____
_____

Date: _____ Action: _____
Result: _____
_____

9

Good Cause, Great Rewards

"The life of a man consists not in seeing visions and in dreaming dreams, but in active charity and in willing service."
- Henry Wadsworth Longfellow

Every week, in every city, numerous charitable events occur.

Some are designed to benefit a cause, while others come to the aid of a particular person or family.

Bottom line is this: there are many opportunities for you to remember just how fortunate you really are.

And here is the best part: Your donation is *you*.

Volunteering your time is one of the most amazing gifts you can share. It costs nothing and creates so much value! Your local newspaper or social media Community page likely have announcements of upcoming events.

Perhaps you can contact various charitable organizations.

In the original edition of this book, I wrote this chapter after setting up my DJ equipment for a fundraiser to help in the fight against a disease affecting a local family. That was the best possible investment of my time at that moment.

Experience the joy for yourself!

Actions and Results (The Success Stories)

Date: _____ Action: _____
Result: _____
_____
_____

Date: _____ Action: _____
Result: _____
_____
_____

Date: _____ Action: _____
Result: _____
_____
_____

Date: _____ Action: _____
Result: _____
_____
_____

Date: _____ Action: _____
Result: _____
_____

10

Special Delivery

"The only gift is a portion of thyself"
- Ralph Waldo Emerson

Wherever you live, challenging weather may exist from time to time. Such conditions create an opportunity to extend kindness to a neighbor or friend.

For those inconvenienced by age or health conditions, it may be a challenge just to make it to the mailbox each day.

How easy would it be for you to take a minute to bring the mail, or newspaper, to their door? Perhaps their garbage cans could also use an escort from the street to the garage.

Keep your eyes open. Look for other helpful tasks, especially during inclement weather. The opportunities are there, awaiting your initiative.

A few moments of your time could mean the world to those around you.

Make a special delivery today!

Actions and Results (The Success Stories)

Date: _____ Action: _____
Result: _____
_____
_____

Date: _____ Action: _____
Result: _____
_____
_____

Date: _____ Action: _____
Result: _____
_____
_____

Date: _____ Action: _____
Result: _____
_____
_____

Date: _____ Action: _____
Result: _____
_____

11

Words Are Worth a Thousand Pictures

"The soul never thinks without a mental picture"
- Aristotle

As someone who has kept a journal for nearly three decades, I can say that this title is very true. When written properly, a thought from today can vividly rekindle wonderful memories years into the future.

Hard-bound journals often cost less than twenty dollars, and some even come with a lock (to help keep your private thoughts even *more* private).

When you are writing, let there be no limits on your hopes and dreams. Deliver them from your heart and mind to the world through your pen (even if the world never gets to see them).

Document your blessings. Be sure to use as many positive, descriptive words as possible

Down the road, when you read back through this year's writings, you may be delighted by the mental pictures dancing in your memory. Even more important, you may be amazed by how you actually predicted your life by sharing your dreams…with *yourself*.

It's your life. It is worth remembering. Jot it down.

Make it last forever.

Actions and Results (The Success Stories)

Date: _____ Action: _____
Result: _____
_____
_____

Date: _____ Action: _____
Result: _____
_____
_____

Date: _____ Action: _____
Result: _____
_____
_____

Date: _____ Action: _____
Result: _____
_____
_____

Date: _____ Action: _____
Result: _____
_____

12

Enjoy Thanksgiving Every Day

"A thankful heart is not only the greatest virtue, but the parent of all other virtues."
- Cicero

Before you read this title and make a break for the grocery store for stuffing and candied yams, that is not the intent of this action step.

It is geared toward the true meaning of Thanksgiving, which is giving thanks.

No huge meal, no football, no tryptophan-induced naps.

Despite what we may believe, we all have *something* to be thankful for, every day. Start small when naming your blessings.

You have the eyes to read these words. If someone holds a door open, say thank you. When someone blesses you after a sneeze, be appreciative. For larger gestures, take time to send a thank-you note or card. Express gratitude with a phone call. Share a meal (turkey or otherwise).

Be thankful, be appreciative.

Happy Thanksgiving!

Actions and Results (The Success Stories)

Date: _____ Action: _____
Result: _____
_____
_____

Date: _____ Action: _____
Result: _____
_____
_____

Date: _____ Action: _____
Result: _____
_____
_____

Date: _____ Action: _____
Result: _____
_____
_____

Date: _____ Action: _____
Result: _____
_____

13

Have a Laugh!

"Laughter is the sun that drives winter from the human face."
- Victor Hugo

Have you ever enjoyed a laugh-attack that starts with something simple and innocent and ends with you rolling on the floor, tears streaming down your cheeks?

As I write this, I am smiling a mile wide because I have been lucky enough to experience *many* of these.

How long has it been since *you* experienced such laughter? I don't mean just a chuckle, chortle or guffaw, but a hysterical rock-solid oh-my-gosh-my-ribs-are-gonna-hurt-tomorrow laugh-riot?

If you really have to strain to remember, stop thinking and jump-start the *next* one. Watch your favorite funny movie. Hop on-line and re-discover clips from your favorite comedians.

Re-connect with an old friend who loves to laugh.

Check the local paper and find a comedy show this weekend!

Laughter is all about connecting with a moment, finding the humor and letting loose. Try it today. It's infectious.

Who knows? Your next laugh may just start a chain reaction.

Actions and Results (The Success Stories)

Date: _____ Action: _____
Result: _____
_____
_____

Date: _____ Action: _____
Result: _____
_____
_____

Date: _____ Action: _____
Result: _____
_____
_____

Date: _____ Action: _____
Result: _____
_____
_____

Date: _____ Action: _____
Result: _____
_____

14

Get Back in the Game

*"Man is most nearly himself when he achieves
the seriousness of a child at play."
- Heraclitus*

In hindsight, I enjoyed a very active lifestyle as a child. Between Little League baseball, gym class at school and weekends playing in the yard, I was a healthy kid with a great deal of social interaction.

Drive past a playground these days, and you will likely see fewer kids out there being active. This is not a slam on the younger generation, but the statistics on overweight and socially-disconnected children may be worth mentioning.

At the time of this writing, I am well into my fifty-second year. While Little League baseball has been replaced by Hey-I'm-Middle-Aged softball, I still enjoy taking the field. The action, teamwork, cheering and laughing are magic. It still feels great to leave the real world behind and be part of the action!

Was there a game you enjoyed as a child? Get out there and play it again. Chances are there may be an opportunity nearby, which includes people your own age. In researching this action step, I actually discovered a local softball league in search of players sixty years and older!

Play like a kid again. Get back in the game.

Actions and Results (The Success Stories)

Date: _____ Action: _____
Result: _____
_____
_____

Date: _____ Action: _____
Result: _____
_____
_____

Date: _____ Action: _____
Result: _____
_____
_____

Date: _____ Action: _____
Result: _____
_____
_____

Date: _____ Action: _____
Result: _____
_____

15

Park It Right Here

"Generosity is not giving me that which I need more than you do, but it is giving me that which you need more than I do."
- Kahlil Gibran

My wife Tina has a term for the premium parking spots closest to a mall or shopping center, just beyond the medical-necessity area. She refers to them as *'princess parking'*. I laughed the first and, if I recall, the second and third time I heard her exclaim "Ooh, look, princess parking!" as we pulled in.

One day as we were shopping, she began to pull into one of these solid-gold spots and noticed another car approaching, driven by an elderly woman. While there were no markings on her vehicle signaling that she required special parking, Tina backed up, waved the woman toward the spot, and found a different one for us.

The woman's smile and wave let us know just how much she appreciated this gesture. What a feeling that was! The action cost us nothing and it made a big difference in this woman's day.

We all park our cars nearly every day. Try this action once and I'll bet you will look for even more opportunities to share princess parking!

Actions and Results (The Success Stories)

Date: _____ Action: _____
Result: _____
_____
_____

Date: _____ Action: _____
Result: _____
_____
_____

Date: _____ Action: _____
Result: _____
_____
_____

Date: _____ Action: _____
Result: _____
_____
_____

Date: _____ Action: _____
Result: _____
_____

16

Don't Keep the Change

"He who allows his day to pass by without practicing generosity and enjoying life's pleasures is like a blacksmith's bellows – he breathes but does not live."
- Sanskrit Proverb

If my football-shaped bank is any indication, this country has a seriously heavy amount of pocket change floating around. For a recent visit to the coin-counting machine, I nearly had to ask a friend to help me carry it into the store.

That trip led to the creation of this action step. Gather your loved ones and seek out a local family who may be experiencing a financial challenge. Churches are a great place to look. Then put the name of your beneficiary on a box, bottle, or jar in which you will put your spare change every day. At the end of a predetermined amount of time, cash in the coins, buy a general-purpose gift certificate for groceries, gas or home needs, and deliver it (anonymously, if possible) to the person or family.

Imagine the value of giving that you can instill in your family members! Even better, your kind gesture may just trigger a chain reaction, inspiring the person receiving your gift to pay it forward someday.

Actions and Results (The Success Stories)

Date: _____ Action: _____
Result: _____
_____
_____

Date: _____ Action: _____
Result: _____
_____
_____

Date: _____ Action: _____
Result: _____
_____
_____

Date: _____ Action: _____
Result: _____
_____
_____

Date: _____ Action: _____
Result: _____
_____

17

Share Your Expertise

"A teacher affects eternity; he can never tell where his influence stops."
- Henry Brooks Adams

Is there something in your life at which you excel? It could be your job, a sport, an activity, or a craft. Whatever it is, someone once took the time to teach you.

Perhaps now would be the perfect time for you to share that knowledge and talent with a person who is striving to learn or improve.

Imagine being the person who teaches a young athlete to throw a perfect spiral, or a curve-ball. Have you ever heard the excited "I did it!" yell of a child who has just learned how to ride a bike?

How incredible a feeling will it be when you help teach someone, child or adult, to read. A new world will open to that mind, and you will have shared the key. Perhaps there is a community education program for which you can volunteer.

Not sure what to do? Keep your eyes and ears open.

Opportunities are everywhere.

Actions and Results (The Success Stories)

Date: _____ Action: _____
Result: _____
_____
_____

Date: _____ Action: _____
Result: _____
_____
_____

Date: _____ Action: _____
Result: _____
_____
_____

Date: _____ Action: _____
Result: _____
_____
_____

Date: _____ Action: _____
Result: _____
_____

18

The Gift of Music

*"Music washes away from the soul
the dust of everyday life."
- Berthold Auerbach*

Music is a connection which many people in the world feel. Whether you play an instrument, possess singing talent, simply hum along, clap to the beat or just enjoy listening to music, you have an opportunity to share a special moment.

At the time of the original writing of this book, my grandfather lived in a wonderful Veterans home, and people often stopped by to play piano, guitar or harmonica. The Army Band graced their beautiful garden for patriotic celebrations. During the holidays, groups of children paraded through singing cheerful carols.

As a DJ, I occasionally schedule a drop-in visit at a local retirement community to play their favorite songs. My compensation consists of laughter, hugs and the amazing stories the residents share with me, which always proves to be a tremendously enriching experience.

Is there an opportunity for you to share the gift of music with someone who could use a bit of joy?

Do it once, and I bet you will want to share your song again and again.

Actions and Results (The Success Stories)

Date: _____ Action: _____
Result: _____
_____
_____

Date: _____ Action: _____
Result: _____
_____
_____

Date: _____ Action: _____
Result: _____
_____
_____

Date: _____ Action: _____
Result: _____
_____
_____

Date: _____ Action: _____
Result: _____
_____

19

The Power of Praise

"There is no investment you can make which will pay you so well as the effort to scatter sunshine and good cheer through your establishment."
- Orison Swett Marden

As a busy self-employed individual, I am often on the road enjoying meetings with clients. Whenever possible, I schedule them at one of my favorite sandwich shops. Time and time again, I receive my order with a smile and kind greetings from the staff.

Recently, after returning to my office, I took ten minutes to craft a letter to their manager. I singled out my regular servers by name, mentioning why they are each special to me.

Even brighter smiles awaited me on my next visit. They had each received a copy of the letter and had been praised mightily by the manager at that week's team meeting. A few simple words, acknowledging *their* efforts, meant the world to these wonderful people. That letter was worth its weight in gold.

Is there someone in your life who is deserving of this gesture?

Improve the world for that person (and yourself) today.

Invest in the power of praise!

Actions and Results (The Success Stories)

Date: _____   Action: _____
Result: _____
_____
_____

Date: _____   Action: _____
Result: _____
_____
_____

Date: _____   Action: _____
Result: _____
_____
_____

Date: _____   Action: _____
Result: _____
_____
_____

Date: _____   Action: _____
Result: _____
_____

20

Capture the Moment, Make It Last Forever

"Memory is the diary that we all carry around with us."
- Oscar Wilde

A friend was recently telling me about his dream car. It is beautiful, it is powerful, it is expensive…and he only gets to drive it a few months per year.

Last winter, he was missing the car, big time. We discussed a way for him to enjoy that behind-the-wheel feeling anytime he desires.

His first ride of the spring will have a co-pilot in the back seat.

He will be setting up his camera on a tripod, capturing the action through the windshield. After a quick save to his laptop, he will forever have an exciting show to watch, complete with the sound of his modified engine spitting out close to four-hundred horsepower.

Is there a dream ride in *your* life? Or another experience that you'd love to be able to tap into (and enjoy) anytime you wish?

Bring your camera and catch the action, with yourself as the star.

Watch it over and over. It'll be the best rerun you've ever seen!

Actions and Results (The Success Stories)

Date: _____ Action: _____
Result: _____
_____
_____

Date: _____ Action: _____
Result: _____
_____
_____

Date: _____ Action: _____
Result: _____
_____
_____

Date: _____ Action: _____
Result: _____
_____
_____

Date: _____ Action: _____
Result: _____
_____

About the Author

Steve Gamlin enjoys life as a professional speaker, author, former radio personality and stand-up comedian, living with his wife Tina in a small town in New Hampshire.

For anyone who has not experienced the four seasons of New England weather, you're really missing something wonderful. Since February 1968, Steve has slogged through the rain and mud of spring, roasted under the summer sun, raked enough fall leaves to fill a dozen dump trucks, and moved enough winter snow to earn the Silver Shovel Award (if there was such a thing)...and he wouldn't trade one minute of it.

Through it all, Steve has enjoyed a journey of learning and experience, many trials and challenges, including the highest highs of accomplishment and the lowest lows of failure...which taught him to always shake off the ashes and bounce back even higher.

It has been an amazing, award-winning journey as an entertainer, author, comedian, and professional speaker. More valuable than any accolade is the collection of amazing family, friends and clients whom he treasures.

Thank you for reading this little book. Steve hopes it will bring as much pleasure to you as a reader as it has for him as the author.

Best wishes to you for an incredible life that always keeps a great big smile on your face and in your heart.

We hope you have enjoyed the tips, strategies and actionable items found within your copy of **"20 to Life (In a Good Way)!"**

Are you ready for more? Want to keep building up, moving forward and redefining success in your life?

We do, and we have made it very simple to take this next step.

Aim your smartphone camera at the QR Code below.

Your device should ask you if you wish to go there.

Say YES...and we'll see you on the inside!

https://www.MotivationalFirewood.com/products

Actions and Results (The Success Stories)

Date: _____ Action: _____

Result: _____

_____

_____

Date: _____ Action: _____

Result: _____

_____

_____

Date: _____ Action: _____

Result: _____

_____

_____

Date: _____ Action: _____

Result: _____

_____

_____

Date: _____ Action: _____

Result: _____

_____

Actions and Results (The Success Stories)

Date: _____ Action: _____
Result: _____
_____
_____

Date: _____ Action: _____
Result: _____
_____
_____

Date: _____ Action: _____
Result: _____
_____
_____

Date: _____ Action: _____
Result: _____
_____
_____

Date: _____ Action: _____
Result: _____
_____

Actions and Results (The Success Stories)

Date: _____ Action: _____

Result: _____

_____

_____

Date: _____ Action: _____

Result: _____

_____

_____

Date: _____ Action: _____

Result: _____

_____

_____

Date: _____ Action: _____

Result: _____

_____

_____

Date: _____ Action: _____

Result: _____

_____

Actions and Results (The Success Stories)

Date: _____ Action: _____
Result: _____
_____
_____

Date: _____ Action: _____
Result: _____
_____
_____

Date: _____ Action: _____
Result: _____
_____
_____

Date: _____ Action: _____
Result: _____
_____
_____

Date: _____ Action: _____
Result: _____
_____

Actions and Results (The Success Stories)

Date: _____ Action: _____

Result: _____

_____

_____

Date: _____ Action: _____

Result: _____

_____

_____

Date: _____ Action: _____

Result: _____

_____

_____

Date: _____ Action: _____

Result: _____

_____

_____

Date: _____ Action: _____

Result: _____

_____

Actions and Results (The Success Stories)

Date: _____ Action: _____
Result: _____
_____
_____

Date: _____ Action: _____
Result: _____
_____
_____

Date: _____ Action: _____
Result: _____
_____
_____

Date: _____ Action: _____
Result: _____
_____
_____

Date: _____ Action: _____
Result: _____
_____

Actions and Results (The Success Stories)

Date: _____ Action: _____
Result: _____
_____
_____

Date: _____ Action: _____
Result: _____
_____
_____

Date: _____ Action: _____
Result: _____
_____
_____

Date: _____ Action: _____
Result: _____
_____
_____

Date: _____ Action: _____
Result: _____
_____

Actions and Results (The Success Stories)

Date: _____ Action: _____
Result: _____
_____
_____

Date: _____ Action: _____
Result: _____
_____
_____

Date: _____ Action: _____
Result: _____
_____
_____

Date: _____ Action: _____
Result: _____
_____
_____

Date: _____ Action: _____
Result: _____
_____

Actions and Results (The Success Stories)

Date: _____ Action: _____

Result: _____

_____

_____

Date: _____ Action: _____

Result: _____

_____

_____

Date: _____ Action: _____

Result: _____

_____

_____

Date: _____ Action: _____

Result: _____

_____

_____

Date: _____ Action: _____

Result: _____

_____

Actions and Results (The Success Stories)

Date: _____ Action: _____
Result: _____
_____
_____

Date: _____ Action: _____
Result: _____
_____
_____

Date: _____ Action: _____
Result: _____
_____
_____

Date: _____ Action: _____
Result: _____
_____
_____

Date: _____ Action: _____
Result: _____
_____

www.ingramcontent.com/pod-product-compliance
Lightning Source LLC
LaVergne TN
LVHW041346080426
835512LV00006B/648